middle School

Word M

Es
W

# MATH

NEW LEAF

**New Leaf Education**
P. O. Box 16230
Baltimore, Maryland 21210

New Leaf Education has a special offer on new products
for people on our mailing list.
Go to www.newleafeducation.com to learn more.

*Design and Cover Illustration:*
Ophelia M. Chambliss
Oliver Bliss Design

Printed in the United States of America

10  9  8  7  6  5  4  3  2  1

# Contents

# welcome to the

**Essential Words**

# MATH

## GLOSSARY!

## ABOUT THE BOOK

Here is a glossary to help you learn the Essential Words in Math that you will need to be successful in school. These Essential Words will also help you succeed on state tests. There are more than 200 Math words in the book! They are listed in alphabetical order under seven main topics.

## Here is a sample word with its features:

**Easy-to-read definitions**

### coordinates
The numbers in an ordered pair that tell the location of a point on the coordinate plane. For example, the coordinates for the ordered pair (2, 3) are 2 and 3.

**Art to help understanding**

*First coordinate—tells how far to move left or right from the origin.*
↓
*(2, 3)*
↑
*Second coordinate—tells how far to move up or down from the origin.*

**Example in context**

We hope that you will find this book easy to use and enjoyable. Tell us what you think. We would love to hear from you!
www.newleafeducation.com

# DATA ANALYSIS & PROBABILITY

## bar graph

A graph that uses rectangles (bars) to display data.
A bar graph compares data sets.

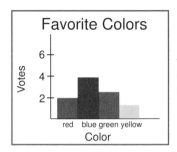

*In this example, we are comparing number of votes for each color.*

## bias sample

A sample where the responses favor some outcomes more than others.

*Question: Should the school pay for band uniforms?*

*Bias sample: Ask only students in the band.*

*Random sample: Ask every fourth student in the school.*

## circle graph

A graph that uses sectors of a circle to display data.
A circle graph shows data as it relates to a whole.

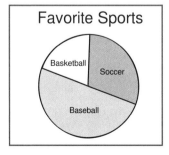

*In this example, we are looking at a certain sport – soccer– as it relates to the three sports shown.*

## combination

A grouping of items in which order does not matter.

Joe  Sue  Ed

*Choose 2 people from the 3.*

  or   or
Joe  Sue       Sue  Ed         Joe  Ed

*Because you want to choose two people, the order you choose them does not matter.*

 and   *Choosing Joe and Sue is one combination.*
Joe        Sue

## data

Information or facts.

> *Heights of basketball players, colors of T-shirts, and ages of your family members are all examples of data.*

## dependent event

When one event happening affects the probability of another event happening.

> *Event 1 – Pick a green marble without looking in the bag.* **Do not replace it in the bag.**
>
> *Event 2 – Pick a green marble without looking.*
>
> *Event 2 is **dependent on** Event 1 because the number of marbles changes.*

# DAtA ANALySiS & PRoBABiLity

## event

One or more outcomes of an experiment. When flipping a coin, an event can be flipping heads on the coin.

## experimental probability

Probability based on actual results of an experiment or study.

| Age of Students on Soccer Team | | |
|---|---|---|
| Age | Number of Students | Frequency |
| **11** | IIII | **4** |
| 12 | ЖНТ III | 8 |
| 13 | ЖНТ ЖНТ I | 11 |
| 14 | II | 2 |
| | **TOTAL** | **25** |

*There are 25 students on the soccer team; 4 students are 11 years old. The experimental probability of picking an 11-year-old student on the soccer team is $\frac{4}{25}$.*

## frequency table

A table that displays the number of times each item occurs in a data set.

| Age of Students on Soccer Team | | |
|---|---|---|
| Age | Number of Students | Frequency |
| 11 | IIII | 4 |
| 12 | ЖНТ III | 8 |
| 13 | ЖНТ ЖНТ I | 11 |
| 14 | II | 2 |
| | Total | 25 |

*A frequency table is best used to track number of occurences.*

# DATA ANALYSIS & PROBABILITY

## histogram

A bar graph that shows the number of times data items occur within certain ranges.

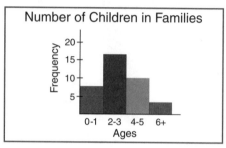

Number of Children in Families

*A histogram is best used for data given in ranges.*

## independent event

When one event happening does not affect the probability of another event happening.

Event 1 – Pick a green marble without looking in the bag. **Replace it in the bag**.

Event 2 – Pick a green marble without looking.

Event 2 is **independent** of Event 1 because the number of marbles is the same on both picks.

## line graph

A graph that uses line segments to show how data changes over time.

Daily Temperature

*A line graph is best used to show change over time.*

## line plot

A number line with symbols above each group to indicate the number of data items in the group.

*X's or other shapes can be used.*

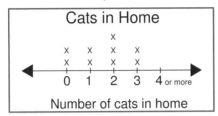

*A line plot is best used to show number of data in each group.*

## lower quartile

The median of the lower "half" of a set of data.

*$Q_1$ is used to abbreviate the lower quartile.*

$Q_1$
Lower Quartile

1, 3, (4,) 5, 5, [6,] 7, 7, 8, 8, 8

Lower half of data    Median

## mean

The sum of the numbers in a set of data divided by the number of numbers in that set.

DATA: *4, 2, 7, 7, 3, 1*

Sum of numbers: *4 + 2 + 7 + 7 + 3 + 1 = 24*
Number of numbers in set: *6*
Mean: *24 ÷ 6 = 4*

*The mean is sometimes called the arithmetic average or average.*

## median

The middle data value when a set of data is arranged from least to greatest.

> **Example A:** *4, 2, 7, 8, 3*
> *Arrange the values from least to greatest. 4 is the median.*
>
> 2, 3, ④, 7, 8
> ↑
> Median

> **Example B:** *9, 4, 7, 3, 5, 8*
> *Arrange the values from least to greatest.*
>
> 3, 4, 5, 7, 8, 9
> ↑
> middle values
>
> *Average: 5 + 7 = 12;*
> *12 ÷ 2 = 6*
> *6 is the median.*

When there is an even number of numbers, the median will be the mean of the two middle numbers.

## mode

The number or numbers that occur most often in a set of data.

> **Example A:** *3, 5, 9, 8, 7, 6, 7*
> *Mode: 7 (It occurs twice.)*
>
> **Example B:** *3, 4, 5, 3, 7, 4, 8*
> *Modes: 3 and 4  (Each occurs twice.)*
>
> **Example C:** *2, 9, 5, 6, 4*
> *Mode: none (No value occurs more than once.)*

## outcome

Any of the possible results that can happen in a probability experiment.

*The outcomes are picking a green marble or picking a yellow marble.*

## outlier

A data point that is very different from other data in a group.

*A survey of the teachers' ages at a local school showed the following results:*

*24, 24, 26, 30, 32, 36, 40, 65*

*Age 65 is the outlier.*

## permutation

A grouping of items in which order matters.

Joe      Sue      Ed

*You want to choose a president and vice president.*

       *or*
Joe   Sue                            Sue   Joe
*president   vice president       president   vice president*

*Because you want to choose 2 people for different positions, order does matter.*

      *or*
Joe   Sue              Sue   Joe

*Joe and Sue or Sue and Joe are two permutations.*

---

## population
The entire group to be studied.

*All the students in a school are the school's student population.*

## probability
A number that describes how likely an event is to occur.

*The probability of picking a green marble is $\frac{3}{4}$ because there are 3 green marbles and 4 marbles total.*

## random sample
A sample where every member in a population has an equal chance of being selected for the purposes of a study.

> *If the names of all the students in a class are put in a hat, and 4 names are selected without looking, then those 4 names make up a random sample for the class. The class is the population.*

## range
The difference between the greatest data value and the least data value in a set of data.

> ***Data:*** *14, 16, 16, 19, 21, 24, 28, 28, 35*
>
> *Greatest Data Value: 35*
> *Least Data Value: 14*
> *Range: 35 − 14 = 21*

# DATA ANALYSIS & PROBABILITY

## sample

A part of the population used for a study.

*Population: All the students in your school.*

*Sample: Ten students from your school.*

## scatter plot

A graph that displays two sets of data as ordered pairs.

*A scatter plot is used to see if there is a relationship between the two sets of data.*

## set

A collection of things.

$$\{\,1,\,2,\,3\,\}$$
$$\{\,A,\,B,\,C\,\}$$
$$\{\,\star,\,\blacklozenge,\,\blacktriangle\,\}$$

## stem-and-leaf plot

A data display that uses place value to break apart data values.

*A stem-and-leaf plot is often used to organize large data sets. The ages of the teachers are 28, 29, 31, 32, 32, 41, 43, 50.*

### Teacher Ages

| Stem | Leaf |
|------|------|
| 2 | 8 9 |
| 3 | 1 2 2 |
| 4 | 1 3 |
| 5 | 0 |

2|8 = 28 years old

## tree diagram

An organized display of all possible combinations or outcomes.

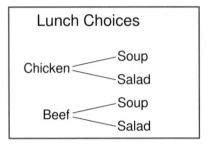

The 4 possible combinations shown are:

(chicken & soup),

(chicken & salad),

(beef & soup),

(beef & salad).

## upper quartile

The median of the upper "half" of a set of data.

*The upper quartile can be written as $Q_3$.*

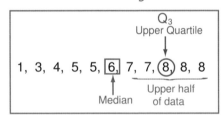

## Venn diagram

A diagram that shows how groups are related.

*Sara and Paul are just on the soccer team.*
*Megan and Elana are on both the soccer and baseball teams.*
*Pilar and Mike are just on the baseball team.*

# Geometry & Measurement

## acute angle

An angle that is greater than 0° and less than 90°.

## acute triangle

A triangle with each angle less than 90°.

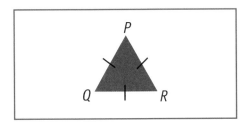

## adjacent angles

Angles that have a common point and a common side.

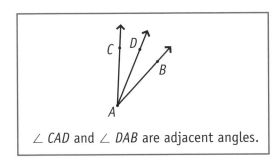

∠ CAD and ∠ DAB are adjacent angles.

*∠CAD is adjacent to (next to) ∠DAB.*

# Geometry & Measurement

## angles

Figures formed by two rays that have the same endpoint.

∠ *stands for "angle."*

*m∠ stands for "the measure of an angle."*

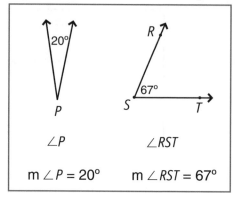

∠P        ∠RST

m∠P = 20°     m∠RST = 67°

## area

The number of square units needed to fill the space inside a two-dimensional figure.

*Area is measured in square units such as square inches (in.²) or square meters (m²).*

The area of the rectangle is 8 square units.

## base (of a solid figure)

A flat surface of a solid figure that helps to describe the type of solid figure.

*The base of a cone is a circle.*

*The base of a square pyramid is a square.*

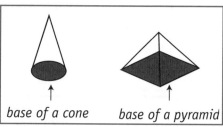

base of a cone     base of a pyramid

# Geometry & Measurement

## capacity

The amount a container can hold.

*The capacity for this container is 1 quart.*

## center (of a circle)

The point that is the same distance from every point on a circle.

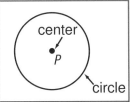

## circle

The set of points that are all the same distance from a single point called the center.

*The symbol ⊙ is used for "circle." Circles are named by their centers.*

*This is ⊙ G. Every point on ⊙ G is 5 units from the center.*

## circumference

The distance around a circle.

*The letter C stands for circumference.*

## complementary angles

Two angles whose measures add to 90°.

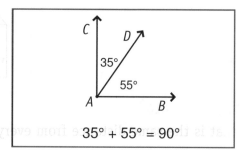

$$35° + 55° = 90°$$

*∠CAD and ∠DAB are complementary.*

$$23° + 67° = 90°$$

*∠R and ∠S are complementary.*

## cone

A solid with one circular base and a vertex.

## congruent

Having the same size and shape.

*The symbol ≅ is read "is congruent to."*

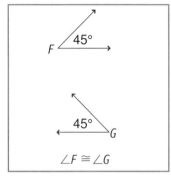

$\angle F \cong \angle G$

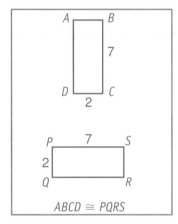

$ABCD \cong PQRS$

$$\overline{WX} \cong \overline{YZ}$$

# Geometry & Measurement

## corresponding angles (of paired polygons)
Matching angles of polygons.

*Corresponding angles have the same measure and are in the same position in each polygon.*

*∠B and ∠F,*

*∠A and ∠E,*

*∠C and ∠G,*

*∠D and ∠H*

*are corresponding angles.*

## corresponding angles (of lines)
Angles that are in matching positions when a line intersects two other parallel lines.

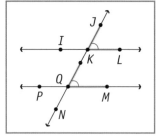

*∠JKL and ∠JQM,*
*∠LKN and ∠MQN,*
*∠JKI and ∠JQP,*
*∠IKN and ∠PQN*
*are corresponding angles.*

## cube
A solid figure with six congruent square faces.

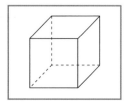

## customary system
A system for measuring length, capacity, weight, and temperature.

*Some basic units are:*
*Inch (in.)*
*Cup (c)*
*Pound (lb)*
*Degree Fahrenheit (°F)*

# Geometry & Measurement

## cylinder

A solid figure with two parallel bases that are congruent circles.

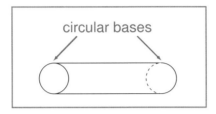

circular bases

## degree (angles)

A unit used to measure angles.

*The symbol for degree is °.*

*The measure of ∠A is 120 degrees or 120°.*

## diameter

A line segment that passes through the center of a circle and has endpoints on the circle.

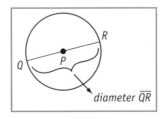

diameter $\overline{QR}$

$\overline{QR}$ *is a diameter of circle P.*

## edge

Where two faces of a solid figure meet.

*$\overline{BC}$ is one of the edges on this cube. Others are $\overline{AD}$, $\overline{DC}$, $\overline{AF}$, $\overline{AB}$, $\overline{FE}$, $\overline{CG}$, $\overline{EG}$, $\overline{BE}$, $\overline{FH}$, $\overline{HD}$, and $\overline{HG}$.*

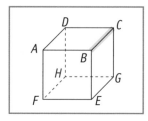

## equilateral triangle

A triangle with three equal sides.

*$\triangle$ ABC is equilateral.*

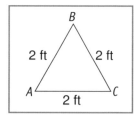

## face (of a solid figure)

A flat surface of a solid figure.

*ABEF is a face of this cube.*

*Other faces are ABCD, BCGE, HFEG, DCGH, and ADHF.*

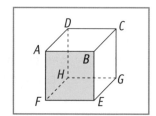

## hexagon

A polygon with six sides.

# Geometry & Measurement

## hypotenuse

The longest side of a right triangle. The hypotenuse is the side opposite the right angle.

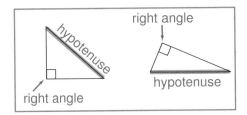

## image

The figure formed by a transformation.

*Image is a reflection of the original.*

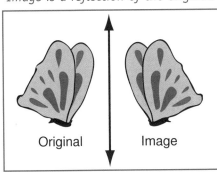

Original     Image

## intersecting lines

Lines that meet in one point.

*Lines m and n are intersecting. They meet at point P.*

## isosceles triangle

A triangle with at least two equal sides.

## legs (of a right triangle)

The two shorter sides of a right triangle.

## length

The distance of something from beginning to end.

*The length of the trip to the school is 2 miles.*

## line

A collection of points that form a never-ending straight path in opposite directions.

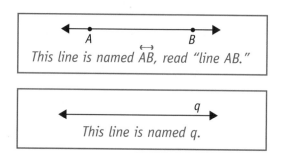

*This line is named $\overleftrightarrow{AB}$, read "line AB."*

*This line is named q.*

# Geometry & Measurement

## line of symmetry

Any line that can divide a figure into two mirrored, congruent parts.

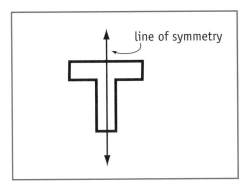

line of symmetry

## line segment

The part of a line that connects two points.

$\overline{YZ}$ = 1 inch

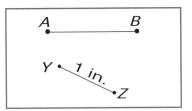

A      B

Y   1 in.

Z

## metric system

A system of measuring based on the decimal system.

Some basic units:

Meter

Liter

Gram

Degree Celsius (°C)

## net

A two-dimensional figure that can be folded to form a solid figure.

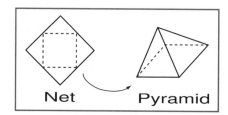

Net        Pyramid

## obtuse angle

An angle with a measure greater than 90° and less than 180°.

## obtuse triangle

A triangle with one obtuse angle.

## octagon

A polygon with eight sides.

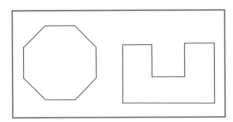

## parallel lines

Lines in the same plane that never meet.

*The symbol || is read*
*"is parallel to."*

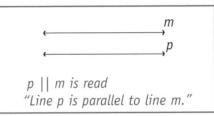

p || m is read
"Line p is parallel to line m."

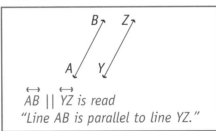

$\overleftrightarrow{AB}$ || $\overleftrightarrow{YZ}$ is read
"Line AB is parallel to line YZ."

## parallelogram

A quadrilateral with two pairs of parallel sides.

$\overline{AB}$ || $\overline{DC}$    $\overline{AD}$ || $\overline{BC}$

$\overline{WX}$ || $\overline{ZY}$    $\overline{WZ}$ || $\overline{XY}$

$\overline{JK}$ || $\overline{ML}$    $\overline{JM}$ || $\overline{KL}$

## pentagon

A polygon with five sides.

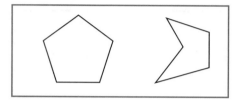

## perimeter

The distance around a polygon.

*The letter p usually stands for perimeter.*
*To find the perimeter of a polygon, add the lengths of all the sides.*

*6 + 6 + 4 + 4 + 4 = 24 inches*

## perpendicular lines

Two lines that intersect to form a 90°, or a right angle.

*The symbol ⊥ is read "is perpendicular to."*

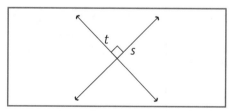

*t ⊥ s   Line t is perpendicular to line s.*

# Geometry & Measurement

## pi

The ratio of the circumference of a circle to the length of its diameter.

*The symbol for pi is π .*

*π = 3.14159....*

*The estimated values for pi are 3.14 and $\frac{22}{7}$ .*

## plane

A flat surface with no thickness that extends forever in all directions.

*Think of the surface of your desk extending in all directions.*

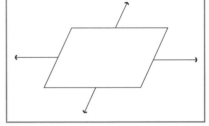

## point

A location that has no size.

## polygon

A closed figure formed by three or more line segments that do not cross (or intersect).

## polyhedron

A three-dimensional solid figure in which all the faces are polygons.

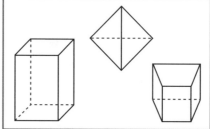

## prism

A three-dimensional solid with one pair of congruent, parallel, polygon faces.

*A prism is named for the shape of its base.*

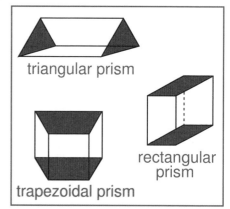

triangular prism

trapezoidal prism

rectangular prism

## pyramid

A three-dimensional solid with triangular faces that meet at a point called a vertex.

*Pyramids are named for the shape of their bases.*

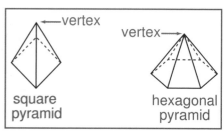

vertex

vertex

square pyramid

hexagonal pyramid

# Geometry & Measurement

## Pythagorean theorem

In any right triangle, the sum of the squares of the lengths of the legs is equal to the square of the length of the hypotenuse.

$a^2 + b^2 = c^2$

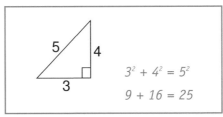

## quadrilateral

A polygon with four sides.

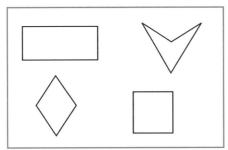

## radius

A line segment that connects the center to the circle.

*The letter r is typically used to represent the length of the radius.*

*r = 2 inches*

$\overline{MG}$ *is the radius of circle M.*

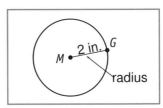

---

**Math**  **Essential Words Glossary**  **27**

## ray

A part of a line that starts at one endpoint and extends forever in one direction.

*The symbol for a ray is* $\longrightarrow$ .

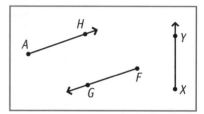

$\overrightarrow{AH}$ *is read "ray AH."*
$\overrightarrow{YX}$ *is read "ray YX."*
$\overrightarrow{FG}$ *is read "ray FG."*

## rectangle

A parallelogram with four right angles.

## reflection

A transformation that flips a figure over a line to produce a mirror image.

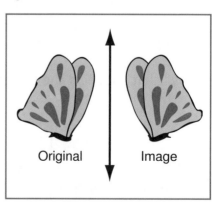

*A reflection is sometimes called a flip.*

Original          Image

# Geometry & Measurement

## regular polygon

A polygon in which all sides are the same measure and all angles are the same measure.

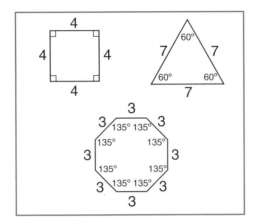

## rhombus

A parallelogram with four sides of equal length.

## right angle

Any angle with a measure of 90°.

$m\angle A = 90°$.
$m\angle DEF = 90°$.

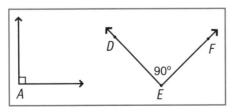

*The measure of angle A is 90°.*
*The measure of angle DEF is 90°.*

**Math**  **Essential Words Glossary**  **29**

## right triangle

A triangle with one right angle.

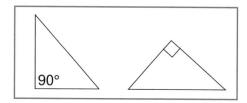

## rotation

A transformation that turns a figure about a fixed point.

*A rotation is also sometimes called a turn.*

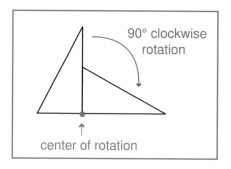

## rotational symmetry

The ability to turn a figure less than 360° around the center and match the original figure.

*This figure has rotational symmetry.*

# Geometry & Measurement

## scale factor

The ratio of corresponding lengths for similar figures.

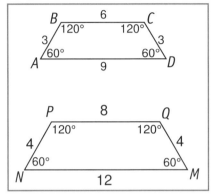

*The scale factor of ABCD to NPQM is 3:4 or $\frac{3}{4}$.*

## scalene triangle

A triangle with no sides of the same length.

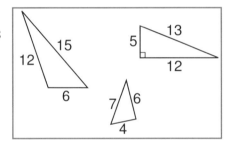

## similar figures

Two figures with congruent corresponding angles and proportional corresponding side lengths.

*The symbol ~ is read "is similar to."*

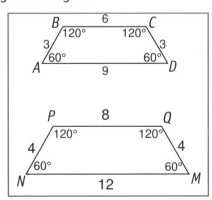

*ABCD ~ NPQM is read "ABCD is similar to NPQM."*

---

## skew lines

Lines that lie in different planes and are neither parallel nor intersecting.

*$\overleftrightarrow{BC}$ and $\overleftrightarrow{AE}$ are one pair of skew lines.*

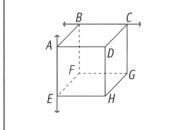

## sphere

The set of all points in space that are the same distance from a given point (center).

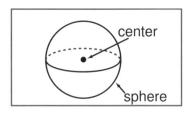

## square

A parallelogram with four right angles and four congruent sides.

## straight angle

Any angle with a measure of 180°.

*A line forms a straight angle.*

# Geometry & Measurement

## supplementary angles

Two angles whose measures add to 180°.

$60° + 120° = 180°$

$140° + 40° = 180°$

## surface area

The sum of the areas of all the surfaces.

*Top: 6 x 10 = 60*
*Bottom: 6 x 10 = 60*
*Front: 10 x 4 = 40*
*Back: 10 x 4 = 40*
*Sides: 4 x 6 = 24*

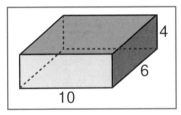

*60 + 60 + 40 + 40 + 24 + 24 = 248 square units*
*Surface area = 248 square units*

## tessellation

A repeating pattern of shapes that completely covers a plane.

## transformation

A change in position, shape, or size of a figure.

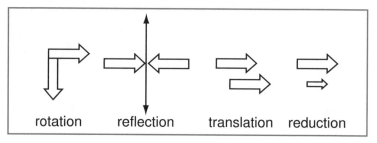

rotation    reflection    translation    reduction

## translation

A transformation that slides each point of a figure the same distance and in the same direction.

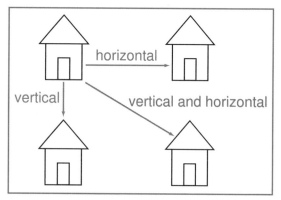

horizontal

vertical

vertical and horizontal

*A translation is sometimes called a slide.*

## trapezoid

A quadrilateral with only one pair of parallel sides.

# Geometry & Measurement

## triangle

A polygon with three sides.

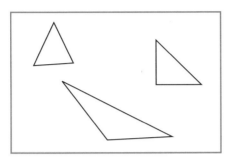

## vertex

The point of intersection of sides at their endpoints.

*Each vertex is circled.*

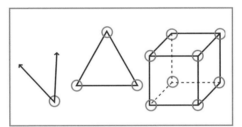

## vertical angles

Angles formed by two intersecting lines.

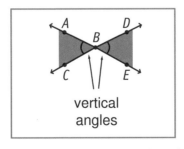

vertical
angles

*∠ABC and ∠DBE are vertical angles.*
*∠CBE and ∠ABD are also vertical angles.*

---

## volume

The number of cubic units needed to fill the space inside a three-dimensional solid.

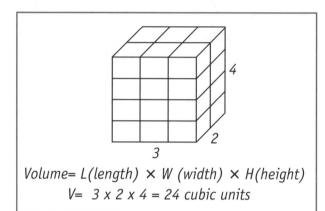

*Volume= L(length) × W (width) × H(height)*
*V= 3 x 2 x 4 = 24 cubic units*

## weight

A measure that tells how heavy something is.

*The weight of a book is 2 pounds.*

## absolute value

The distance a number is from zero (0) on a number line.

*The symbol | | is read "the absolute value of."*

> The number 3 is 3 units from zero on the number line.
>
> $|3| = 3$    The absolute value of 3 is 3.
>
>
>
> The number -2 is 2 units away from zero on the number line.
>
> $|-2| = 2$    The absolute value of -2 is 2.

## Associative Property of Addition

For three or more numbers, their sum is always the same. It does not matter how the numbers are grouped.

*In algebraic notation, this property is written:*
*For any numbers a, b, and c, (a+b)+c = a+(b+c).*

> $(4 + 2) + 8 = 4 + (2 + 8)$
> $\phantom{(4+2}6\phantom{)} + 8 = 4 + \phantom{(}10$
> $\phantom{(4+2)+}14 = 14 ✔$

## Associative Property of Multiplication

For three or more numbers, their product is always the same. It does not matter how the numbers are grouped.

*In algebraic notation, this property is written:*
*For any numbers a, b, and c, (ab)c = a(bc).*

> $(2 × 5) × 8 = 2 × (5 × 8)$
> $\phantom{(2×5}10\phantom{)} × 8 = 2 × \phantom{(}40$
> $\phantom{(2×5)×}80 = 80 ✔$

---

## base (of an exponent)

A number that is used as a factor. (The exponent tells how many times to use the base as a factor.)

$$3^4 \leftarrow \text{exponent}$$

$$\uparrow$$
base

The exponent is 4.
The base 3 is used as a factor 4 times.

$$3^4 = 3 \times 3 \times 3 \times 3 = 81$$

## common factor

A number that is a factor of two or more numbers.

Factors of 8: 1, 2, 4, 8

Factors of 12: 1, 2, 3, 4, 6, 12

Common factors of 8 and 12: 1, 2, 4

## Commutative Property of Addition

Numbers can be added in any order without changing the answer.

This property is written algebraically as:
For any numbers a and b, a + b = b + a.

$$3 + 5 = 5 + 3$$
$$8 = 8 ✔$$

## Commutative Property of Multiplication

Numbers can be multiplied in any order without changing the answer.

This property is written algebraically as:
For any numbers a and b, a × b = b × a.

$$3 \times 5 = 5 \times 3$$
$$15 = 15 ✔$$

# Number Sense & Operations

## compatible numbers

Numbers that make calculation easy.

*You can estimate using compatible numbers.*

> *120 and 6 are compatible numbers. 120 ÷ 6 = 20.*
>
> *To estimate 125 ÷ 5.8, you can use compatible numbers.*
>
> $$120 ÷ 6 = 20,$$
> *So, 125 ÷ 5.8 ≈ 20.*

## composite numbers

Whole numbers greater than 1 that have more than two whole number factors.

> *Composite numbers: 4, 6, 9*
>
> *Factors of 4: 1, 2, 4 because 1 × 4 = 4; 2 × 2 = 4*
>
> *Factors of 6: 1, 2, 3, 6 because 1 × 6 = 6; 2 × 3 = 6*
>
> *Factors of 9: 1, 3, 9 because 1 × 9 = 9; 3 × 3 = 9*

## denominator

The bottom number in a fraction.

> $\frac{3}{4}$ ←*denominator*

## difference

The answer to a subtraction problem.

> $6 - 2 = 4$
> *difference*

## Distributive Property

Multiply a single term by two or more terms inside parentheses.

*For any numbers a, b, and c, this property is written algebraically in two forms:*

$a (b + c) = a × b + a × c$   $a (b - c) = a × b - a × c$

$3 (4 + 5) = 3 × 4 + 3 × 5$   $3 (6 - 2) = 3 × 6 - 3 × 2$

$3 (9) = 12 + 15$   $3 (4) = 18 - 6$

$27 = 27$   $12 = 12$

## divisible

Can be divided by a number with no remainder.

| | |
|---|---|
| *6 is divisible by 3.* | *6 ÷ 3 = 2 remainder 0* |
| *7 is NOT divisible by 3.* | *7 ÷ 3 = 2 remainder 1* |

## estimate

An educated guess.

*An estimate can be used when you don't need an exact answer.*
*A good estimate for 9.98 x 2 is 20 because 10 x 2 = 20.*

## expanded form

A way to write numbers using base 10.

*You rewrite the digits with the proper place value. For 345,*

| *hundreds* | *tens* | *ones* |
|---|---|---|
| *3* | *4* | *5* |

$3 \times 100 + 4 \times 10 + 5 \times 1$

$3 \times 10^2 + 4 \times 10^1 + 5 \times 10^0$ *Expanded form uses base 10.*

*The expanded form of 345 is $3 \times 10^2 + 4 \times 10^1 + 5 \times 10^0$*

## exponent

Tells how many times a base is used as a factor.

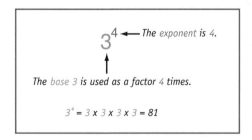

$3^4$ ← *The exponent is 4.*

*The base 3 is used as a factor 4 times.*

$3^4 = 3 \times 3 \times 3 \times 3 = 81$

# Number Sense & Operations

## factor

A number that is multiplied by another number to find a product.

> 3 and 4 are factors of 12.
>
> $3 \times 4 = 12$

## factor tree

A diagram that shows the prime factors of a number.

*There may be more than one factor tree for a number.*

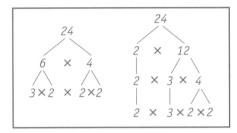

## fraction

A number in the form $\dfrac{a}{b}$ , where b cannot be equal to zero.

*Fractions are usually used to compare a number of parts to the whole.*

$$\frac{1}{2}, \quad -\frac{5}{6}, \quad \frac{x}{4} \quad \text{are all fractions.}$$

## greatest

The largest number or quantity.

*25, 8, 16*

*25 is the greatest number.*

## greatest common factor

The common factor that is greater than any other common factor.

*The greatest common factor is often abbreviated as GCF.*

> *Factors of 12: 1, 2, 3, 4, 6, 12*
> *Factors of 8: 1, 2, 4, 8*
>
> *The common factors of 12 and 8 are: 1, 2, 4*
> *The greatest common factor of 12 and 8 is 4.*

## Identity Property of One for Multiplication

The product of any number and one is that number.

*This property is written algebraically as:*

$a \times 1 = a$ or $1 \times a = a$.

> *5 × 1 = 5*
> *1 × 24 = 24*
> *356 × 1 = 356*

## Identity Property of Zero for Addition

The sum of any number and zero is that number.

*This property is written algebraically as:*

$a + 0 = a$  or $0 + a = a$.

> *5 + 0 = 5*
> *0 + 12 = 12*
> *276 + 0 = 276*

## improper fraction

A fraction in which the numerator is greater than or equal to the denominator.

> $\frac{12}{8}$ *is an improper fraction.*    $\frac{7}{7}$ *is an improper fraction.*
>
> *12 > 8*                                      *7 = 7*

## integers

The set of positive whole numbers, their opposites, and 0.

> *The set of integers is:*
> *{..., -4, -3, -2, -1, 0, 1, 2, 3, 4, ....}*

## inverse operations

Any pair of operations that undo each other.

*Inverse operations:*

| addition and subtraction | multiplication and division |
|---|---|
| *3 + 4 = 7* | *5 × 2 = 10* |
| *7 − 4 = 3* | *10 ÷ 2 = 5* |

## irrational numbers

Numbers that cannot be written as the ratio of two integers.

*In decimal form, an irrational number cannot be written as a decimal that repeats or ends.*

> *$\pi$ and $\sqrt{2}$ are irrational numbers.*
> *$\pi$ = 3.1415926.....   $\sqrt{2}$ = 1.4142135.....*
> *Approximations for $\pi$ and $\sqrt{2}$ are:*
> *$\pi \approx 3.14$    $\sqrt{2} \approx 1.41$*

## least

The smallest number or quantity.

*16, 8, 3, 7*

*3 is the least number.*

## least common denominator

Least common multiple of the denominators of two or more fractions. LCD is often used as an abbreviation for the least common denominator.

$$\frac{5}{6} \quad \frac{9}{10} \quad \frac{2}{15}$$

*In the example, the denominators are 6, 10, and 15.*
*Multiples of 6: 6, 12, 18, 24, **30**, 36, 42, 48, 54, **60**...*
*Multiples of 10: 10, 20, **30**, 40, 50, **60**...*
*Multiples of 15: 15, **30**, 45, **60**...*

*The least common denominator is 30 because the least common multiple is 30.*

## least common multiple

The common multiple that is less than any other common multiple of two or more numbers. The least common multiple is abbreviated as LCM.

*Multiples:*
*8: 8, 16, **24**, 32, 40, **48**, ...*
*12: 12, **24**, 36, **48**, ...*
*Common multiples: **24**, **48***
*LCM: **24***

## mixed number

A number that is formed with an integer and a fraction.

*integer* ⟶ $3\frac{1}{2}$ ⟵ *fraction*

*All of the following are mixed numbers.*

$$3\frac{1}{2}, 14\frac{1}{5}, 5\frac{7}{10}, -1\frac{3}{4}$$

## multiple

A product of natural numbers.

| | |
|---|---|
| 3 × 4 = 12 | 12 is a multiple of 3 and 4. |
| 5 × 6 = 30 | 30 is a multiple of 5 and 6. |

## natural numbers

Set of numbers you use to count.

{1, 2, 3, 4, 5, ...}

Natural numbers are also known as counting numbers.

## numerator

The top number of a fraction.

$$\frac{2}{5} \leftarrow numerator$$

## numerical expression

An expression with only numbers and one or more operation symbols.

3 + 4

4 × 3 ÷ 6

(6 + 5) × 8 – 25

## opposite

A number that is the same distance from zero on a number line as a given number, but on the other side of zero.

-2 and 2 are opposites.
-2 is the opposite of 2.
2 is the opposite of -2.

## order of operations

A list of steps used to calculate an answer.

*Order:*

*Parentheses*
*Exponents*
*Multiplication or Division (left to right)*
*Addition or Subtraction (left to right)*

$4^2 - (5-2) \times 2 + 1$

| | | | |
|---|---|---|---|
| $4^2 -$ | $3$ | $\times 2 + 1$ | *Parentheses* |
| $16 -$ | $3$ | $\times 2 + 1$ | *Exponents* |
| $16 -$ | | $6 + 1$ | *Multiplication* |
| | $10$ | $+ 1$ | *Subtraction (occurs before addition, reading left to right)* |
| | | $11$ | *Addition* |

## pattern

An arrangement of numbers or things that can be described.

*Some patterns:*

☐,▲, ○, ☐,▲, ○...*(square, triangle, circle)*

*2, 4, 6, 8, 10...(even counting numbers)*

*x, $x^2$, $x^3$, $x^4$...(powers of x)*

## perfect square

A number that has exactly two integer factors that are the same.

*4, 9, 16, 25, 36, 49, 64, 81, and 100 are perfect squares.*

$8 \times 8 = 64$, so 64 is
a perfect square.

## place value

Place value is the value of a digit in a number, based on the location of the digit.

*9463.07*

*The value of 4 is 400 (4 hundred) because 4 is in the hundreds place.*

## power

An expression formed by a base with its exponent, or the value of that expression.

> *$3^2 = 9$*
> *$3^2$ is read "three to the second power" or "three squared;"*
> *9 is the second power of three.*

## prime factorization

Writing a composite number as the product of all of its prime factors.

> *$12 = 2 \times 2 \times 3 = 2^2 \times 3$*
> *$39 = 3 \times 13$*
> *$45 = 3 \times 3 \times 5 = 3^2 \times 5$*
> *$16 = 2 \times 2 \times 2 \times 2 = 2^4$*

## prime number

Any whole number with exactly two different factors, 1 and itself.

*Prime numbers are circled.*

> 1 ② ③ 4 ⑤
> 6 ⑦ 8 9 10
> ⑪ 12 ⑬ 14 15
> 16 ⑰ 18 ⑲ 20
> 21 22 ㉓ 24 25

## product

The answer to a multiplication problem.

$$3 \times 4 = 12$$
$$\uparrow$$
$$product$$

## proper fraction

A fraction that is less than 1.

$$\frac{2}{3} \text{ and } \frac{4}{5} \text{ are proper fractions.}$$

## quotient

The answer to a division problem.

$$2\overline{)8}^{\,4} \longleftarrow quotient$$

## rational numbers

Numbers that can be written as a fraction using two integers where the denominator is not 0.

*Some rational numbers are:*

$4, 0.75, -2\frac{1}{2}, 5.1, 0, 0.\overline{3}, \sqrt{4}$

$$4 = \frac{4}{1}$$

$$0.75 = \frac{3}{4}$$

$$-2\frac{1}{2} = -\frac{5}{2}$$

$$5.1 = 5\frac{1}{10} = \frac{51}{10}$$

$$0 = \frac{0}{1}$$

$$0.\overline{3} = 0.333... = \frac{1}{3}$$

$$\sqrt{4} = \frac{2}{1}$$

## real numbers

The set of numbers that includes all rational and irrational numbers.

*Examples of Real Numbers*

$$0.\overline{3},\ \pi,\ -5,\ 2\frac{5}{12},\ -0.95,\ \sqrt{2}$$

## reciprocals

Two numbers that when multiplied give a product of 1.

$$\frac{2}{1} \times \frac{1}{2} = 1 \qquad\qquad -\frac{2}{3} \times -\frac{3}{2} = 1$$

*$\frac{1}{2}$ and 2 are reciprocals.*     *$-\frac{2}{3}$ and $-\frac{3}{2}$ are reciprocals.*

## relatively prime numbers

Any two numbers whose greatest common factor is 1.

*Factors of 27: 1, 3, 9, 27*

*Factors of 35: 1, 5, 7, 35*

*Greatest Common Factor = 1*

*27 and 35 are relatively prime.*

## repeating decimal

Any decimal that has one or more digits that repeat forever.

*A single digit or set of repeating digits can be shown with a bar.*

$$0.333... = 0.\overline{3}$$
$$0.4545... = 0.\overline{45}$$
$$0.625625625... = 0.\overline{625}$$

## scientific notation

A shorthand way of writing very large or very small numbers. A number written as a product so that the first factor is greater than 1 and less than 10, and the second factor is a power of 10.

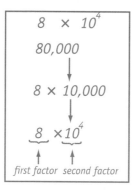

$8 \times 10^4$

80,000

↓

$8 \times 10,000$

↓

$\underbrace{8}_{\text{first factor}} \times \underbrace{10^4}_{\text{second factor}}$

*To write 80,000 in scientific notation, first rewrite it in expanded form:*

*8 × 10,000.*

*Continue using a power of 10.*

## sequence

An ordered set of numbers.

> *1, 2, 3, 4, ...*
>
> *−4, −2, 0, 2, 4, ...*

## simplest form (of a fraction)

A fraction written so that the numerator and denominator have no common factors other than 1.

> $\frac{3}{12}$ *is not in simplest form.*
> *3 and 12 have a*
> *common factor of 3.*
>
> $$\frac{3}{12} = \frac{3 \div 3}{12 \div 3} = \frac{1}{4}$$
>
> $\frac{1}{4}$ *is the simplest form of* $\frac{3}{12}$.

## simplify

To rewrite something in its simplest form.

> *Simplify: 3 × 8 − 2*
>
> *Simplest form: 22*

> *Simplify:* $\frac{12}{14}$
>
> $\frac{12}{14} = \frac{6}{7}$
>
> *Simplest form:* $\frac{6}{7}$

## square root

One of two equal factors of a number.

*The symbol for square root is* $\sqrt{\phantom{x}}$ .

> *25 = 5 × 5, so the square root of 25 is 5.* $\sqrt{25} = 5$.
>
> $\sqrt{4} = 2,\ \sqrt{36} = 6,\ \sqrt{64} = 8,\ \sqrt{100} = 10$

## standard form

A way of writing a number using digits and place value.

*Everyday numbers like the ones below are written in standard form.*

> *0.258*
>
> *3.1*
>
> *25*
>
> *2,457,598*

## sum

The answer to an addition problem.

> *3 + 5 = 8*
>
> ↑
>
> *sum*

## term (of a pattern)

A number in a pattern.

> 1, 2, 4, 8, 16, ...
>
> Each of the numbers listed above is a term.

## terminating decimal

A decimal that ends.

> 0.548    0.1    2.375

## whole numbers

Zero and all the natural numbers.

> The set of whole numbers is
> {0,1,2,3,4...}.

## Zero Property of Multiplication

The product of any number and zero is zero.

This property is written algebraically as:

$a \times 0 = 0$ or

$0 \times a = 0.$

> $3 \times 0 = 0$
>
> $14 \times 0 = 0$

## cross product

The product of two numbers that are diagonal from each other in a ratio.

$$\frac{3}{4} \times \frac{9}{12} \qquad \frac{x}{4} \times \frac{7}{2}$$

$$3 \times 12 = 4 \times 9 \qquad 2(x) = 4 \times 7$$
$$x = 14$$

## discount

The amount subtracted from the price of an item.

$$\$15 - \$10 = \$5$$
$$\uparrow$$
$$discount$$

## equivalent fractions

Fractions that have the same value.

| Equivalent Fractions | NOT Equivalent Fractions |
|---|---|
| $\dfrac{3}{12}, \dfrac{25}{100}$ | $\dfrac{3}{5}, \dfrac{12}{24}$ |
| both equal $\dfrac{1}{4}$. | |
| $\dfrac{3}{12} \div \dfrac{3}{3} = \dfrac{1}{4}$ | $\dfrac{12}{24} = \dfrac{1}{2}$ |
| $\dfrac{25}{100} \div \dfrac{25}{25} = \dfrac{1}{4}$ | $\dfrac{3}{5} \neq \dfrac{1}{2}$ |

## interest

The amount paid for borrowing money or earned by lending money.

*You pay interest on a loan, but you earn interest from money in a savings account.*

## percent

A ratio that compares a number to 100.

*The symbol for percent is %. "Per" means "for" and "cent" means "hundred." 72% is read seventy-two percent and means 72 per 100 or 72/100.*

## principal

An amount of money borrowed or deposited.

*When you put $100.00 in the bank for savings, the $100.00 is the principal.*

*When you borrow $15,000 to buy a car, the $15,000 is the principal.*

## proportion

An equation showing that two ratios are equal.

$$\frac{1}{2} = \frac{4}{8}$$

$$\frac{x}{25} = \frac{3}{5}$$

## rate

A ratio that compares two quantities measured in different units.

*25 miles in 4 hours*
*50 words per minute*
*7 points/game*

# RAtio, PROpoRtioN, & PeRceNt

## ratio

A comparison of two quantities using division.

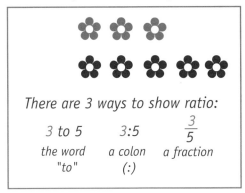

*There are 3 ways to show ratio:*

| 3 to 5 | 3:5 | $\dfrac{3}{5}$ |
|--------|-----|----------------|
| *the word "to"* | *a colon (:)* | *a fraction* |

## scale

A ratio that compares dimensions in a drawing to the actual dimension.

*The scale of the living room drawing is 2 cm = 10 ft.*

## scale drawing

A drawing that shows a real object smaller than or larger than the actual object. Uses a scale to show size relationships.

## scale model

A model of a real object that is smaller than or larger than the actual object.

*Dollhouses and toy cars are scale models.*

## unit rate

A rate in which the number in the denominator is one.

$$\frac{65 \text{ miles}}{1 \text{ hour,}} \qquad \frac{85 \text{ words}}{1 \text{ minute,}} \qquad \frac{15 \text{ feet}}{1 \text{ second}}$$

# EQUATIONS & INEQUALITIES

## Addition Property of Equality

If the same number is added to each side of an equation, the results are equal.

*The property is written in algebraic form for all numbers a, b, and c: if a = b, then a + c = b + c.*

$$3 = 3$$
$$3 + 4 = 3 + 4$$
$$7 = 7$$

*If a = b, then a + 2 = b + 2.*

$a = b$

$a+2 = b+2$

## Division Property of Equality

If you divide each side of an equation by the same nonzero number, the sides remain equal.

*The property is written in algebraic form for all numbers a, b, and, c and c does not equal 0: if a = b, then $\dfrac{a}{c} = \dfrac{b}{c}$ .*

$$12 = 12$$
$$12 \div 3 = 12 \div 3$$
$$4 = 4$$

If $3x = 24$

then $\dfrac{3x}{3} = \dfrac{24}{3}$

$x = 8$

Division Property of Equality

## equation

A mathematical statement stating that two quantities are equal.

*The symbol = is called the equal sign and is read "equals" or "is equal to."*

> *2 + 1 = 3*
>
> *3x + 6 =12*
>
> *2(a+b) = 3c + 4d*

## formula

A rule that shows a relationship between quantities.

*A is area; l is length; w is width*

*Area = length x width*

*A = lw is a formula for the area of a rectangle.*

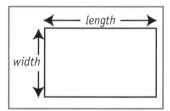

## inequality

A mathematical sentence that uses one of the following symbols to state a relationship between two quantities:

$<$ *is less than*

$>$ *is greater than*

$\leq$ *is less than or equal to*

$\geq$ *is greater than or equal to*

$\neq$ *is not equal to*

> *3 + x < 5*
>
> *3 plus x is less than 5.*
>
> *4 ≥ -2*
>
> *4 is greater than or equal to -2.*
>
> *3 ≤ 3*
>
> *3 is less than or equal to 3.*
>
> *7 ≠ 6*
>
> *7 is not equal to 6.*

# EQUATIONS & INEQUALITIES

## Multiplication Property of Equality

If each side of an equation is multiplied by the same number, the sides remain equal.

*The property is written in algebraic form for all numbers a, b, and c:*   *if a = b, then a × c = b × c.*

$$2 = 2$$
$$2 × 3 = 2 × 3$$

$$\frac{x}{2} = 5$$
$$2 \left(\frac{x}{2}\right) = 2 \,(5)$$

## solution

Any value that makes an equation or inequality true.

*x + 2 = 6*
*4 + 2 = 6*
*4 is a solution of the equation*
*x + 2 = 6 because 4 + 2 = 6.*
*y > 0*

*5, 8, and 10 are some of the solutions of the inequality y > 0 because 5, 8, and 10 are all greater than 0. Other solutions include any number greater than 0. There are infinitely many solutions.*

## Subtraction Property of Equality

If the same number is subtracted from each side of an equation, the results are equal.

*The property is written in algebraic form for all numbers a, b, and c:*
*if a = b, then a − c = b − c.*

$$8 = 8$$
$$8 − 2 = 8 − 2$$
$$6 = 6$$

$$\frac{a \;=\; b}{\triangle}$$
$$\frac{a − 5 = b − 5}{\triangle}$$

## algebraic expression

An expression with only numbers, variables, operation symbols, and no equal sign.

$$9x^2 - 18x + 1$$

$$1 + \frac{a}{2}$$

## binomial

A polynomial with only two terms.

$$x + 4$$

$$2y + 3z$$

## coefficient

A number that is multiplied by a variable.

$$9\,x^2 - 18\,x + 1$$

$9$, $-18$, and $1$ are all coefficients.

## like terms

Terms with the same variable factors.

Like terms:

$$9x^2, \; 2x^2$$

Not like terms:

$$9x^2, \; 18x$$

$x$ is squared in the first term, but not in the second term.

# VARIABLES & EXPRESSIONS

## monomial

A number, variable, or a product of numbers and variables.

$$3, x, -2y, \frac{1}{2}, a^2b$$

## polynomial

A monomial or sum or difference of monomials.

$$11x^2 - 18x + 1$$

## simplify (an algebraic expression)

To rewrite an expression so that it has the fewest terms possible.

Simplify:

$2x + 3x + 5y - 3y =$

$5x \quad + \quad 2y$

## term (of a polynomial)

A monomial in a polynomial.

*In the polynomial*

*$9x^2 - 18x + 1,$*

*$9x^2$, $-18x$, and 1 are all terms.*

## variable

A letter used to represent one or more numbers.
The letters $x$ and $a$ are variables.

## coordinates

The numbers in an ordered pair that tell the location of a point on the coordinate plane. For example, the coordinates for the ordered pair (2, 3) are 2 and 3.

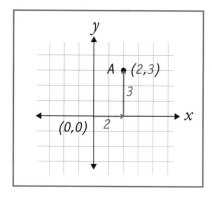

*First coordinate—tells how far to move left or right from the origin.*

↓

*(2, 3)*

↑

*Second coordinate—tells how far to move up or down from the origin.*

## coordinate plane

A plane that is organized by a horizontal number line called the x-axis and a vertical number line called the y-axis.

# Coordinate Plane

## function

A relationship of inputs and outputs so that there is exactly one output for each input.

Example 1

| input | output |
|-------|--------|
| 7     | 10     |
| 8     | 11     |
| 12    | 15     |
| 2     | 5      |

Function

| input | output |
|-------|--------|
| 2     | 6      |
| 4     | 5      |
| 2     | 8      |
| 9     | 7      |

Not a Function

*The second table is NOT a function because there are two different outputs (6 and 8) for the input 2.*

Example 2

| At $8 an Hour | |
|---------------|---|
| Hours Worked *(h)* | Paid *(p)* |
| 2 | $16 |
| 3 | $24 |
| 4 | $32 |

*The number of hours you are paid (p) is a function of hours worked (h). There is exactly one dollar amount (output, p) for each hour worked (input, h).*

## linear function

A function that has the shape of a line when graphed on the coordinate plane.

*Function: y = 2x + 1*

# COORDINATE PLANE

### ordered pair

A pair of numbers that gives the position of a point on the coordinate plane.

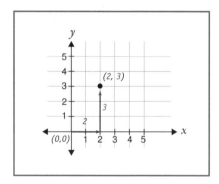

*(2,3) is an ordered pair.*

### origin

The point where the x-axis and y-axis of a coordinate plane cross.

# COORDINATE PLANE

## quadrant

The four sections of the coordinate plane.

*Quadrants are numbered with Roman numerals (I, II, III, IV).*

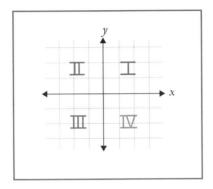

## reflection

A transformation that flips a figure over a line to produce a mirror image.

# COORDINATE PLANE

## rotation

A transformation that turns a figure about a fixed point.

## slope

A ratio that describes the steepness of a line in the coordinate plane.

*Slope is represented by the variable m and is often referred to as "rise over run."*

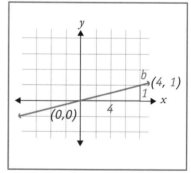

$$\text{Slope of line } a = \frac{rise}{run} = \frac{(y_2 - y_1)}{(x_2 - x_1)} = \frac{4 - 0}{2 - 0} = \frac{4}{2} = 2$$

$$\text{Slope of line } b = \frac{rise}{run} = \frac{(y_2 - y_1)}{(x_2 - x_1)} = \frac{1 - 0}{4 - 0} = \frac{1}{4}$$

*The slope of line a is 2, which is greater than the slope of line b, $\frac{1}{4}$.*
*Line a is taller, or "steeper," than line b.*
*Slope measures the "steepness" of a line.*

# COORDINATE PLANE

## slope-intercept form

A linear equation written in the form $y = mx + b$, where $m$ represents slope and $b$ represents the $y$-intercept.

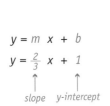

$y = m\ x\ +\ b$

$y = \frac{2}{3}\ x\ +\ 1$

slope  y-intercept

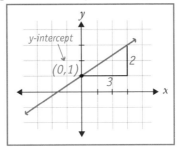

## translation

A transformation that slides each point of a figure the same distance and in the same direction.

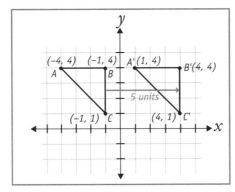

## x-axis

The horizontal number line in the coordinate plane.

## x-coordinate

The first number in an ordered pair that tells how far from (0,0) to move left or right. In the ordered pair (2,3), 2 is the x-coordinate.

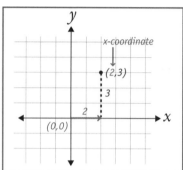

## x-intercept

The x-coordinate of the point where a line crosses the x-axis.

*The coordinates for the x-intercept are (−3,0).*

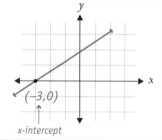

## y-axis

The vertical number line in the coordinate plane.

# COORDINATE PLANE

## y-coordinate

The second number in an ordered pair that tells how far from (0,0) to move up or down. In the ordered pair (2,3), 3 is the y-coordinate.

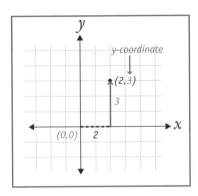

## y-intercept

The y-coordinate of the point where a line crosses the y-axis.

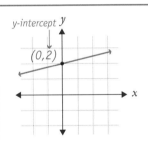

*The coordinates for the y-intercept are (0,2).*

# Reference Chart

## LENGTH

### Metric

1 kilometer = 1,000 meters

1 meter = 100 centimeters

1 centimeter = 10 millimeters

### Customary

1 mile = 1,760 yards

1 mile = 5,280 feet

1 yard = 3 feet = 36 inches

1 foot = 12 inches

## CAPACITY

### Metric

1 liter = 1,000 milliliters

### Customary

1 cup = 8 ounces

1 pint = 2 cups

1 quart = 2 pints

1 gallon = 4 quarts

## MASS AND WEIGHT

### Metric

1 gram = 1,000 milligrams

1 kilogram = 1,000 grams

### Customary

1 pound = 16 ounces

1 ton = 2,000 pounds

## TIME

1 minute = 60 seconds

1 hour = 60 minutes

1 year = 12 months

1 week = 7 days

1 day = 24 hours

1 year = 365 days

# Reference Chart

## PERIMETER

*square*

$s$  $P= 4s$

*rectangle*

$w$  $P= 2l + 2w$  *or*  $P= 2(l + w)$

$l$

## CIRCUMFERENCE

*circle*

$C = 2\pi r$  *or*  $C = \pi d$

## AREA

*square*

$s$  $A= s^2$

$s$

*rectangle*

$w$  $A= lw$

$l$

*parallelogram*

$h$  $A= bh$

$b$

---

**Math**                    **Essential Words Glossary**          **71**

# Reference Chart

triangle

 $A = \frac{1}{2} bh$   or   $A = \frac{bh}{2}$

trapezoid

 $A = \frac{1}{2} h (b_1 + b_2)$

circle

 $A = \pi r^2$

## VOLUME

cube

surface area

$V = s^3$   $S.A. = 6s^2$

rectangular prism

surface area

 $V = lwh$   $S.A. = 2(lw) + 2(hw) + 2(lh)$

cylinder

surface area

$V = \pi r^2 h$   $S.A. = 2\pi rh + 2\pi r^2$

# Reference Chart

Pi                    π                         π ≈ 3.14   or   π ≈ 22/7

## Degree (temperature)

*A unit used to measure temperature.*

*Different scales like Celsius and Fahrenheit can be used to measure temperature. The temperature on this thermometer is 0°C or 32°F.*

$$F = \frac{9}{5} C + 32$$

$$C = \frac{5}{9} (F - 32)$$

# INDex

# INDex